Growing
Closer
to God

DICK PURNELL

HARVEST HOUSE PUBLISHERS

EUGENE, OREGON

Unless otherwise indicated, all Scripture quotations are taken from the HOLY BIBLE, NEW INTERNATIONAL VERSION®. NIV®. Copyright©1973, 1978, 1984 by the International Bible Society. Used by permission of Zondervan. All rights reserved.

Cover by The Dugan Group, Bloomington, Minnesota

GROWING CLOSER TO GOD
Copyright © 2005 by Dick Purnell
Published by Harvest House Publishers
Eugene, Oregon 97402
www.harvesthousepublishers.com

ISBN-13: 978-0-7369-1509-0
ISBN-10: 0-7369-1509-5

All rights reserved. No part of this publication may be reproduced, stored in a retrieval system, or transmitted in any form or by any means—electronic, mechanical, digital, photocopy, recording, or any other—except for brief quotations in printed reviews, without the prior permission of the publisher.

Printed in the United States of America

07 08 09 10 11 12 13 / BP-KB / 10 9 8 7 6 5 4 3

Dedicated to Dad and Mom,
who are both now with the Author of the Word in heaven.

*One of my favorite early memories is of my dad and mom at the
breakfast table, reading the Bible and praying each day. I always
respected them for that. The sense of importance they felt for God's
Word influenced me to make the Bible central in my own life.
Through the years, their example has given me the desire to
diligently study and live according to the Word of God.*

Contents

Our Greatest Need

ↄ€

As we look at our lives, we become aware of many desires and needs we long to see fulfilled. These needs might include happiness, security, love, good health, purpose in life, peace of mind, and many others. The list seems endless.

However, the greatest need we will ever have on this earth is to know God intimately. A deep relationship with Him will affect every area of our lives and actually transform us into the persons He wants us to be.

In our busy world with all its stresses and pressures, it is easy to neglect God and live most of the time as if He doesn't exist. But we desperately need to have a close relationship with Him. Jesus said, "I am the vine; you are the branches. If a man remains in me and I in him, he will bear much fruit; apart from me you can do nothing" (John 15:5). Without Him, we lack the power of God and can do nothing to please Him.

That God desires our fellowship is probably one of the most amazing revelations expressed in the Bible. Its significance is overwhelming! The heavenly Father, infinite God, wants to establish and develop an intimate relationship with us! In John 4:23 Jesus states, "Yet a time is coming and has now come when the true worshipers will worship the Father in spirit and truth, for they are the kind of worshipers the Father seeks."

Reflect on this amazing truth—the Lord of glory wants us to understand Him as much as the human mind can comprehend! But we must seek Him. The benefits are tremendous as we learn to live and view life from His perspective. "For I know the plans I have for you, declares the LORD, plans to prosper you and not to harm you, plans to give you hope and a future. Then you will call upon me and come and pray to me, and I will listen to you. You will seek me and find me when you seek me with all your heart" (Jeremiah 29:11-13). He floods our minds and fills our hearts with Himself. He keeps His promise, "And my God will meet all your needs according to his glorious riches in Christ Jesus" (Philippians 4:19).

You may be just starting your Christian life and wondering what it is all about. You want something to help you get going. Or maybe you have been struggling for months, even years, to grow in your faith, and it has been an up-and-down experience. You want to develop consistency in your walk with God. Or you may be thoroughly enjoying your fellowship with the Lord and looking for something to help you continue the process of maturing.

In light of the Father's desire for you to seek Him and your great need to know Him intimately, you've decided to embark on a 31-day experiment during which you will learn how to develop a habit of spending quality time each day reading God's Word and praying. You hold in your hands a simple plan to aid your personal growth in building a wonderful relationship with the Lord. It is one book in a dynamic series of devotional guides I call The 31-Day Experiments.

Why do I call each book an experiment? Webster's says an experiment is a trial procedure carried out under controlled conditions in order to discover an unknown effect. I want you to try this experiment of a daily meeting with God. If you do the experiment faithfully for 31 days, you will experience a whole new depth in your relationship with our wonderful Lord. This experiment is a challenge to try something new to see if it works for you, to discover timeless truth, and to apply your discoveries to improve your life and increase your faith.

Take the challenge to grow closer to God. Set out to cultivate your walk with the Lord—to see as He sees, hear as He hears, act as He acts, and feel as He feels. The Bible says, "Taste and see that the LORD is good" (Psalm 34:8). That is a wonderful invitation to experience the living God in your own life.

This is no light exercise. It is a serious matter. All the forces of evil will oppose you. You must have Christ's strength to be victorious. I urge you to begin with the prayer and covenant on the next two pages. The prayer is to ask for God's help, and the covenant is to show your determination.

As you spend time alone with the Lord for the next 31 days, expect Him to richly bless you in your endeavors to develop your relationship with Him. I pray you will grow closer to God not just for one month but for the rest of your life.

My Prayer

Dear Heavenly Father!

You are so magnificent and loving. It is amazing that You want me to know You—intimately. What mercy and compassion!

When I look at my life, I see how self-centered I am. Everything revolves around me and my interests. No wonder I am dissatisfied with the quality of my relationship with You. Only You can change my heart from being self-centered to being Christ-centered.

I am about to start an experiment in which I will endeavor to cultivate my walk with You for the next 31 days. I honestly seek to know You. My whole life, with all my concerns and needs, I now place in Your hands.

Take me now and radically change my life. Because You are infinitely wise and good, I trust You to mold me into the kind of person You desire me to be. Teach me daily about Yourself and Your desires for the way I live.

I am excited and anxious to begin today. Thank You for Your unchanging faithfulness!

In the name of the Lord Jesus Christ. Amen!

Signed_____

Date_____

My Covenant
with God

During the 31 days of this experiment, I promise God that I will diligently work toward deepening my relationship with Him. Today, I make a covenant with God to do the following:

1. Spend 20 to 30 minutes each day in Bible study, prayer, and writing out my thoughts and plans.
2. Ask at least one other Christian to pray daily for me that I will be consistent in doing this experiment. (It would be helpful if that person would do the experiment along with me so that we could share together what we are learning.)
3. Attend a church each Sunday where the Word of God is faithfully proclaimed.

Signed_____

Date_____

Guidelines for Growth

Preparation for Each Day

1. Equipment. Get a Bible that you enjoy reading and a pen to record your thoughts and plans in this book.

2. Time. Choose a specific half hour each day to spend with the Lord. Pick the time of day that is best for you—when your mind is alert and your heart is most receptive to meeting with God.

3. Place. Find a special place where you can clear your mind of distractions and focus your full attention on God and His Word. Suggestions: bedroom, office, school library, living room, outdoors.

Read (10–20 Minutes)

1. Pray earnestly before you begin. Ask the Lord to teach you what He desires you to learn this day. Anticipate meeting with Him.

2. Read the entire passage that is the selection for the day.

3. Read it again, looking for important ideas.

4. Make written notes in this book under the following daily sections:

>   A and B—Study the passage thoroughly to answer the questions. Observe what God says about Himself and how people can live dynamic, godly lives. As you discover more of His truth, your understanding of God's purposes for you will increase.
>
>   C—Write out your personal responses to the Scripture passage you have studied. How, specifically, are you going to apply the lessons you have learned to your life?

5. Choose a verse from the passage you just read that is especially meaningful to you. Copy it onto a card and read it several times during the day. Think about its meaning and impact on your life. Memorize it when you have free mental time; for example, when you are getting ready in the morning, while you are standing in a line, during lunch, waiting for class to begin, relaxing during a break at work, or walking somewhere.

Need (5 Minutes)

1. Pray that the Lord will give you insight into your own life.

2. Decide what your most pressing personal need is that day. It may be the same as on previous days, or it may be different.

3. Write down your request. The more specific you are, the more specific the answer will be.

4. Earnestly pray during the day for God's provision of an answer. Continue to pray for the need you expressed that

day and for unanswered needs from previous days. As you progress through the experiment, exercise your developing faith. Expect God to do big things in your life.

5. When the Lord answers your specific prayers, record the date and how He met your needs. Periodically review God's wonderful provisions, and thank Him often for His faithfulness. This will greatly increase your faith and confidence in Him.

6. At the end of the month, review all the answers to your prayers. Rejoice in God's goodness to you. Keep praying for the requests that still need answers.

Deed (5 Minutes)

1. Ask God for wisdom and direction to apply the particular passage you have just studied. Plan how you will implement your ideas during that day.

2. Take the initiative to express God's wonderful love to someone. Be a servant. Behind every face there is a drama going on. Tap into at least one person's drama and share what God has been teaching you.

3. As you show kindness toward someone, share with him or her what you have been learning during this experiment. Tell the person about your faith in Christ. Here are some suggestions for genuinely caring for the needs of others:

   a. Provide a meal.

   b. Take care of someone's children for an evening.

   c. Help a friend study for a school test.

    d. Do yard work with a neighbor

    e. Write an encouraging letter.

    f. Start a Bible study.

    g. Teach someone a sports activity or a mechanical skill.

    h. Assist in moving household possessions.

    i. Take someone out to lunch and listen to the needs expressed.

    j. Fix something for a neighbor.

    k. Show interest in another's interests.

    l. Give an honest compliment.

    m. Pray with a friend about a need.

    n. Contribute money to a missions cause.

    o. Visit someone in the hospital or at a retirement home.

Application

1. Write down ideas about how you can put into practice specific instructions found in the passage.

2. Devise a plan to implement your ideas.

Last Thing in the Evening

1. *Read*—Look at the passage again, searching for additional ideas about God and your relationship with Him.

2. *Need*—Pray again for your concerns. Thank the Lord that He will answer in His way and in His time.

3. *Deed*—Record all that the Lord guided you to accomplish that day.

4. *Application*—Review what you wanted to implement that day. How did you see God work through your life?

Doing This Experiment with Others

Ask a friend or a group of friends to do the experiment with you. Look at the section in the back of this book that describes how to do this experiment with other believers, such as a friend, Bible study group, small group, Sunday school class, or whole church. As you do the experiment, pray frequently for one another that God will draw you all closer to Himself. Ask the Lord to unite your hearts together. Encourage each other to be disciplined and faithful in completing the experiment. Share together what you are learning and how God is working in your lives.

The Experiment

31 Days of Growing Closer to God

O God, You are my God,
earnestly I seek you;
my soul thirsts for you,
my body longs for you,
in a dry and weary land
where there is no water.
I have seen you in the sanctuary
and beheld your power and your glory.
Because your love is better than life,
my lips will glorify you.

I will praise you as long as I live,
and in your name I will lift up my hands.
My soul will be satisfied as with the richest of foods;
with singing lips my mouth will praise you.

—PSALM 63:1-5

DAY 1

God's Plan to Provide for My Needs

MATTHEW 6:25-34

Key Verses:

For the pagans run after all these things, and your heavenly Father knows that you need them. But seek first his kingdom and his righteousness, and all these things will be given to you as well (Matthew 6:32-33).

Today's Focus:

God knows your every need, even before you do. As your loving Father, He wants to meet those needs in His way and in His time. And He will, if you seek Him with all your heart.

Read: Praise the Lord for His promises.

A. Why does Christ tell you not to be anxious about your needs?

B. Instead of worrying, what should you do?

C. I will seek His kingdom and His righteousness above everything else because:

Need: Pray for peace in your heart.

My greatest need today is:

The Father in heaven answered my prayer on _____ (date). Here's how:

Deed: Pray for opportunities to tell others about Christ.

Based upon God's provision for my needs, I want to help someone else who has a need. Here is my plan:

*A*pplication

Identify a specific area in your life about which you are anxious. Ask God to show you one thing you can do today to overcome that anxiety. Study John 14:25-27 and Philippians 4:6-7.

DAY 2

God's Promises to His Followers

PSALM 37:1-40

Key Verses:

Trust in the LORD and do good; dwell in the land and enjoy safe pasture. Delight yourself in the LORD and he will give you the desires of your heart (Psalm 37:3-4).

Today's Focus:

Commitment to the Lord requires active participation on your part. As you seek to trust and follow Him, He is faithful to fulfill His promises. Those who go their own way and forsake the Lord will reap the consequences of their rebellion.

Read: Praise God for He is faithful.

A. List all the things the Lord will do for you when you live in a righteous manner.

B. What does it mean to delight yourself in the Lord?

C. I want to live the way the Lord wants me to live because:

Need: Pray to keep His ways.

My greatest need today is:

Praise the Lord! He answered my prayer today _____ (date) in this way:

Deed: Pray to give generously to others.

Because I am committed to obey the Lord, I want to:

*A*pplication

"Do good" (Psalm 37:3) today by thinking of a person you know and secretly doing one thing that will encourage him or her. Write down your plans. Endeavor to bring a smile to that person's face and peace to his or her heart.

DAY 3

Assurance of Eternal Life

1 John 5:1-15

Key Verses:

And this is the testimony: God has given us eternal life, and this life is in his Son. He who has the Son has life; he who does not have the Son of God does not have life (1 John 5:11-12).

Today's Focus:

God's testimony regarding His Son and the eternal life He gives is sure. Because God said it, you can believe it! You don't have to doubt or wonder anymore about your eternal future. You can know for certain that right now you have eternal life.

Read: Praise God for giving you eternal life.

  A. How can you know without a doubt that you have eternal life?

B. Why can you believe what God says?

C. I know I have eternal life because:

Need: Thank God that you can trust Him.

My greatest need today is:

God's answer to my prayer came on _____ (date) by this means:

Deed: Pray for boldness to tell others about God's promises.

Because God's eternal life is in me, I want to:

*A*pplication

How would you define eternal life? Take a few minutes and write down what eternal life means, and how it affects the way you live in this world. Read John 3:16 and John 17:3.

DAY
4

Walk Away Free
and Forgiven

LUKE 7:36-50

Key Verse:

Then Jesus said to her, "Your sins are forgiven" (Luke 7:48).

Today's Focus:

Your sins separate you from God, who is holy and righteous. But when you confess your sins, you are forgiven and free to grow closer to Him.

Read: Praise the Lord that He wants you to know Him.

A. What does love for God have to do with forgiveness of your sins?

B. Why is Jesus the only one who can forgive sins?

C. I know that my sins have been forgiven because:

Need: Pray for greater love for Christ.

My greatest need today is:

It is exciting to see God answer my prayer today _____ (date). This is what He did:

Deed: Pray for compassion to help others who are sinners.

Based on all that Christ has done in my life, I will:

*A*pplication

Take a quiet moment today and examine your heart. Are you clean before God? Confess your sins to the Lord like the woman in today's Scripture passage. Write down other verses that reveal promises of God's forgiveness. Thank Him for forgiving you. You can walk away forgiven and free.

DAY 5

Peace with God

ROMANS 5:1-11

Ꝭ

Key Verses:

> *Therefore, since we have been justified through faith, we have peace with God through our Lord Jesus Christ, through whom we have gained access by faith into this grace in which we now stand. And we rejoice in the hope of the glory of God* (Romans 5:1-2).

Today's Focus:

When tough times come (and they will), you have the assurance that even in the midst of pain and suffering Christ offers you the hope that does not disappoint. You have peace with God. He loves you that much.

Read: Praise the Lord for bringing you back to Himself.

A. List the main ideas given in the passage about:

- Faith

- Hope

- Love

B. How has the death of Christ changed your relationship with God?

C. Because of my relationship with God through faith, I can handle tough times by:

Need: Pray to rejoice in all things.

My greatest need today is:

God is so good! On _____ (date) He provided the answer to my prayer by:

Deed: Praise God for demonstrating His love for you.

Because I want others to have peace with God, I will:

*A*pplication

What are some areas of suffering in your life? Commit them to the Lord. Write down positive things that you will trust God to do through those painful times.

DAY
6

Experiencing the Power of God

Ephesians 3:14-21

Key Verses:

Now to him who is able to do immeasurably more than all we ask or imagine, according to his power that is at work within us, to him be glory in the church and in Christ Jesus throughout all generations, for ever and ever! Amen (Ephesians 3:20-21).

Today's Focus:

God the Father, God the Son, and God the Holy Spirit (the Trinity) are active and personally involved in your life as a believer. It is only possible to live the Christian life with their power and strength.

Read: Pray for enlightenment.

A. List the activities of the Trinity in your life:

Father	Christ	Holy Spirit

B. What does it mean for Christ to dwell in your heart through faith?

C. Because I trust God to strengthen me with power, I will:

Need: Pray to be strengthened with God's power.

My greatest need today is:

God answered my prayer on _____ (date). Here's how:

Deed: Pray for boldness to share with others the news of God's power.

I want the Holy Spirit to give me love and power in order for me to:

*A*pplication

Write a prayer of thanksgiving to the Trinity (God the Father, God the Son, and God the Holy Spirit) for their working in your life. Study Paul's other prayer for the Ephesians in chapter 1, verses 15 through 23.

DAY 7

Living with New Purpose

2 CORINTHIANS 5:11-21

Key Verse:

Therefore, if anyone is in Christ, he is a new creation; the old has gone, the new has come! (2 Corinthians 5:17).

Today's Focus:

When you believed Christ died for you, you received Him into your life and a transformation took place. You became a brand-new person!

Read: Praise God for a new life.

A. What does it mean to be reconciled to God?

B. What are some characteristics of your new life in Christ?

C. I love Christ because:

Need: Pray to live for Christ each day.

My greatest need today is:

Praise the Lord! He answered my prayer today _____ (date) in this way:

Deed: Thank Christ that you are His ambassador.

Because God has committed to me the ministry of reconciliation, I want to:

*A*pplication

Ask a fellow believer how he or she became a new creation in Christ. What changes have come into his or her life? Share what Christ has done in your life. Pray for each other that you will help others become reconciled to God.

DAY 8

Passionately Loving God

Psalm 63:1-11

✿

Key Verse:

> *O God, you are my God, earnestly I seek you; my soul thirsts for you, my body longs for you, in a dry and weary land where there is no water* (Psalm 63:1).

Today's Focus:

When you earnestly and sincerely seek the Lord, you will find Him. He will deeply satisfy your soul so that you will be filled with praise to God.

Read: Earnestly pray to know God more fully.

A. List the attitudes and actions toward God that show love for Him.

B. What does God do for those who seek Him?

C. I rejoice in God because:

Need: Pray to remember the Lord throughout your day.

My greatest need today is:

God's answer to my prayer came on _____ (date) by this means:

Deed: Pray for guidance to encourage others to love God.

I want to help someone else today. Here is my plan:

*A*pplication

Write your own song or poem of praise to the Lord, expressing your desire to know Him more closely. Make it a love letter to God.

DAY
9

Joyful Filling and Overflowing

EPHESIANS 5:15-21

Key Verse:

> *Do not get drunk on wine, which leads to debauchery.*
> *Instead, be filled with the Spirit* (Ephesians 5:18).

Today's Focus:

Even though you live in difficult times, the presence of the Holy Spirit in your life can fill you with great rejoicing! The overflow of His love in you will touch the people you meet today.

Read: Praise God for the Holy Spirit's working in your life.

A. What is the Lord's will for you?

B. Describe the characteristics of a Spirit-filled life.

C. I want to be filled with the Holy Spirit because:

Need: Pray for greater wisdom in using your time today.

My greatest need today is:

I am excited that the Holy Spirit answered my prayer today
_____ (date). This is what He did:

Deed: Pray to give thanks for everything.

Today, I would like the Holy Spirit to lead me to:

*A*pplication

Pray for specific people you know and their needs, asking the Holy Spirit to work in their lives. Ask God to give you opportunities to help them understand how the Holy Spirit can fill them with overflowing joy.

DAY 10

Bearing Fruit and Loving Others

JOHN 15:1-17

Key Verse:

I am the vine; you are the branches. If a man remains in me and I in him, he will bear much fruit; apart from me you can do nothing (John 15:5).

Today's Focus:

Intimacy with Christ: It's the precious result of abiding in Him, loving Him, knowing Him more closely. Within such a relationship comes true fulfillment and purposeful living.

Read: Praise the Lord for His bearing fruit through you.

A. The results of abiding (remaining) in Christ are:

B. How can you show that you are a disciple of Christ?

C. I am determined to remain in Christ because:

Need: Pray to bear much fruit.

My greatest need today is:

The Father is wonderful! On _____ (date) He provided the answer to my prayer by:

Deed: Pray to obey His commandments.

Because I am remaining in Christ, I ask the Father to:

*A*pplication

Write down the fruit you see in your life. Thank the Father for working in you. Ask Him to bear more lasting fruit in you. Plan some opportunities today to show love for others, such as encouraging a friend, communicating with a family member, or witnessing to a coworker.

Guidance from God

PROVERBS 3:1-12

Key Verses:

> *Trust in the LORD with all your heart and lean not on your*
> *own understanding; in all your ways acknowledge him,*
> *and he will make your paths straight* (Proverbs 3:5-6).

Today's Focus:

Because God created you and loves you, He knows what's
best for you. His guidance will protect and provide for you
through all your days on earth.

Read: Praise the Lord for His guidelines for living.

A. List below:

Commands to obey	Promises to claim

B. Why should you fear the Lord and shun evil?

C. I will acknowledge God in all my ways because:

Need: Pray for God to guide you today.

My greatest need today is:

God answered my prayer on _____ (date). Here's how:

Deed: Pray to be more loving and faithful.

I believe God will show me the way to:

*A*pplication

Confess to God any area of your life where you have not been trusting in Him with all your heart. Admit the inadequacies of your own understanding, and make a commitment to acknowledge Him in all areas. Thank Him for setting you on His path for your life.

DAY
12

Living by the Spirit

GALATIANS 5:16-26

Key Verse:

So I say, live by the Spirit, and you will not gratify the desires of the sinful nature (Galatians 5:16).

Today's Focus:

The Holy Spirit will enable you to produce godly fruit in your life. The true Christian life can only be lived by total dependence on the Spirit of God.

Read: Thank God for His provisions for you.

A. Write down the different results of these two ways of living:

Acts of the sinful nature	Fruit of the Spirit

B. How can you gain victory over the desires of your sinful nature?

C. Through the power of the Holy Spirit I will:

Need: Pray that the fruit of the Spirit will be evident in your life.

My greatest need today is:

The Holy Spirit answered my prayer today _____ (date) in this way:

Deed: Pray to help others produce the fruit of the Spirit.

The Holy Spirit is leading me to:

*A*pplication

Pray for the Holy Spirit to replace unrighteous activities you do with His wonderful fruit. Memorize Galatians 5:22-23 and seek to develop those characteristics. Share your prayer requests with a trusted friend. Ask him or her to pray earnestly for you to gain victory in these areas.

DAY 13

Walking in God's Light

1 John 1:1–2:2

Key Verse:

> *But if we walk in the light, as he is in the light, we have fellowship with one another, and the blood of Jesus, his Son, purifies us from all sin (1 John 1:7).*

Today's Focus:

God's light reveals the darkness in our hearts and souls. If we honestly confess every time we sin, He is faithful to forgive us and to restore us to walking in His light. There is no greater way to live.

Read: Praise God for His light.

A. How can you go from walking in darkness to walking in God's light?

B. What are the results of walking in the light of God?

C. On the basis of Jesus Christ's forgiving and cleansing power, I:

Need: Pray to consistently walk in His light.

My greatest need today is:

God's answer to my prayer came on _____ (date) by this means:

Deed: Pray for fellowship with other faithful believers.

As I walk in God's light today, I desire to:

*A*pplication

Ask God to identify any sin in your life that is blocking His light. Write down those sins on a separate sheet of paper. Confess your sins and write out 1 John 1:9 across the paper. Then destroy that paper as a visible reminder of God's forgiveness.

DAY 14

The Pleasure of Pleasing God

COLOSSIANS 1:1-14

Key Verse:

And we pray this in order that you may live a life worthy of the Lord and may please him in every way (Colossians 1:10).

Today's Focus:

Living a life worthy of the Lord should be your greatest goal. Such a life is the result of God's work in you and for you, and it's the only life that brings true and lasting joy.

Read: Praise God for His glorious might.

A. What qualities and attributes can you ask God to put into your life and into the lives of others?

B. What really pleases God?

C. I am determined to please the Lord because:

Need: Pray to be filled with the knowledge of His will.

My greatest need today is:

It is exciting to see God answering my prayer today _____ (date). This is what He is doing:

Deed: Pray for greater endurance and patience.

Based upon the prayer in this passage, I want to encourage someone to:

*A*pplication

Memorize the prayer in Colossians 1:9-14. Pray it daily for yourself and for other people. Put their names in the passage when you pray it for them. Send him or her a note of encouragement today.

DAY
15

Discovering the Source of True Success

JOSHUA 1:1-9

Key Verse:

Do not let this Book of the Law depart from your mouth; meditate on it day and night, so that you may be careful to do everything written in it. Then you will be prosperous and successful (Joshua 1:8).

Today's Focus:

The world's definition of success and God's definition are not the same. Success in God's eyes results from a life lived following Him and obeying His commands. The guarantee of that success is His presence in your life.

Read: Thank the Lord He is with you every day.

A. According to God's viewpoint, success is:

B. When you face huge challenges, how can you be strong and courageous?

C. Because I want to prosper in God's eyes, I will:

Need: Pray the Bible into your mind and heart.

My greatest need today is:

God is wonderful! On _____ (date) He provided the answer to my prayer by:

Deed: Pray for courage to share God's Word with someone today.

I want to demonstrate concern by building up someone else. Here is my plan:

*A*pplication

Three times in today's passage the Lord instructs Joshua to "be strong and courageous." Identify an area of weakness in your life, and ask the Lord to help you to be strong and courageous. Follow His commands so you will succeed in His eyes.

DAY
16

Love That Won't
Let You Go

ROMANS 8:28-39

Key Verses:

> *For I am convinced that neither death nor life, neither angels nor demons, neither the present nor the future, nor any powers, neither height nor depth, nor anything else in all creation, will be able to separate us from the love of God that is in Christ Jesus our Lord* (Romans 8:38-39).

Today's Focus:

Absolutely nothing can separate you from God's love! What security that provides. He reassures you that He will always be with you.

Read: Thank the Lord that He loves you infinitely.

A. What can give you confidence to handle anything that comes into your life?

B. When you face trials and difficult people, what promises of God can help you?

C. As a result of being secure in His eternal love, I can:

Need: Pray for victory over problems.

My greatest need today is:

God answered my prayer on _____ (date)! Here's how:

Deed: Pray for confidence:

Since God freely gave Christ to die for me, I:

Application

What causes you to doubt God's love? Make a list of those things, and then read them into today's verse. For example, "I am convinced that neither my financial difficulties, nor a breakup of a relationship, nor my physical problems will be able to separate me from the love of God...." Then spend time praising the Lord for His faithfulness.

DAY 17

Triumphing over Trials and Temptations

JAMES 1:1-18

Key Verse:

Blessed is the man who perseveres under trial, because when he has stood the test, he will receive the crown of life that God has promised to those who love him (James 1:12).

Today's Focus:

When trials and temptations challenge you, God lovingly provides a way to triumph over them. He offers rewards to those who choose to obey Him. He is the giver of every good and perfect gift.

Read: Praise Him for turning difficulties into joyful experiences.

A. Describe the characteristics of the following:

Trials and temptations	Provisions of God

B. What has God promised to those who persevere under trials?

C. When I am tempted, I will:

Need: Pray for power to overcome trials and temptations.

My greatest need today is:

Praise God! He answered my prayer today _____ (date) in this way:

Deed: Pray for wisdom.

I know a friend who is struggling with a trial or temptation. Here is my plan to help him or her get God's victory:

*A*pplication

Describe how the Lord gave you victory over a particular trial or temptation. Thank Him for His provision of strength and wisdom. Write out a plan to handle a particular trial or temptation in the future.

DAY 18

Settling Your Future So You Can Live Now

1 PETER 1:3-25

Key Verses:

> *Praise be to the God and Father of our Lord Jesus Christ! In his great mercy he has given us new birth into a living hope through the resurrection of Jesus Christ from the dead, and into an inheritance that can never perish, spoil or fade— kept in heaven for you, who through faith are shielded by God's power until the coming of the salvation that is ready to be revealed in the last time* (1 Peter 1:3-5).

Today's Focus:

As a believer, you have been given a "living hope." With confidence and hope you can look beyond your present struggles to a guaranteed future and a treasure from God that will never perish, spoil, or fade. Praise God that we can live for more than just today!

Read: Praise God for your future.

A. Describe the things God has promised you.

B. Why can you set your hope in God?

C. As I look at my life and the future God has promised me, I will:

Need: Pray to be holy.

My greatest need today is:

God's answer to my prayer came on _____ (date) by this means:

Deed: Pray to live your life as a stranger in this world.

I would like to bring God's comfort to somebody in need by:

Application

Describe the best inheritance you can imagine receiving in this life. What would it be worth? How would it feel to be the recipient of such an inheritance? Thank God that your inheritance in Him is far greater than anything you could think or imagine—and it will be eternal!

DAY 19

Rewards of Faith and Creativity

MARK 2:1-12

Key Verses:

> *Some men came, bringing to him a paralytic, carried by four of them. Since they could not get him to Jesus because of the crowd, they made an opening in the roof above Jesus and, after digging through it, lowered the mat the paralyzed man was lying on* (Mark 2:3-4).

Today's Focus:

Christ responds to active, creative faith. When you believe God for His provisions, He is honored and willing to act on your behalf.

Read: Praise God He honors faith.

A. How did the paralyzed man and his friends reveal their faith?

B. Why did Christ heal the paralytic?

C. God is glorified when I:

Need: Pray for creative faith.

My greatest need today is:

It is exciting to see how God answered my prayer today
_____ (date). This is what He did:

Deed: Pray for resourcefulness in helping others.

I, too, want to be creative in helping someone to:

Application

Initiate a conversation today with someone who is facing a problem or concern. Offer to pray right then with him or her. Throughout the day continue to pray about his or her need. Take the initiative to try to solve the situation, if possible.

DAY
20

God Answers Prayers

PSALM 34:1-10

Key Verse:

The lions may grow weak and hungry,
but those who seek the LORD lack no good thing
(Psalm 34:10).

Today's Focus:

God will provide for your needs according to His promises. And because of His care for us, He is worthy of our continual praise. You can pray with confidence that the Lord hears you.

Read: Praise the Lord that He listens when you pray.

A. Describe the following:

My attitudes and actions	God's provisions

B. How will the Lord respond when a person fears (reverences) Him?

C. I praise the Lord in all my circumstances because:

Need: Seek the Lord with your whole heart.

My greatest need today is:

The Lord is good! On _____ (date) He provided the answer to my prayer by:

Deed: Pray that other believers will exalt the Lord with you.

In light of all that the Lord has done in my life, I am looking for an opportunity to:

*A*pplication

Make a list of all the ways the Lord has responded to your prayers. Look back at the previous days in this experiment. What were your requests and how did He answer? Tell someone else, and ask them to exalt His name with you.

Date _____

DAY 21

Confidence to Declare the Truth

ROMANS 1:8-25

Key Verse:

I am not ashamed of the gospel, because it is the power of God for the salvation of everyone who believes (Romans 1:16).

Today's Focus:

The good news of Jesus Christ sets the captives of sin free! The power of that message gives us the confidence to proclaim it to people who don't know the Lord. The gospel is truth that changes lives.

Read: Praise God that the gospel has changed your life.

A. Compare the characteristics of these people:

People without God	People with God

B. What do you think "the righteous will live by faith" means? (Compare Romans 1:17 with Galatians 3:11 and Habakkuk 2:4.)

C. With God in my life, I can confidently speak about salvation because:

Need: Pray to live a righteous life.

My greatest need today is:

God answered my prayer on _____ (date). Here's how:

Deed: Pray for boldness to witness.

Being convinced that people need to hear the gospel, I will actively seek to:

*A*pplication

What differences has God made in your life since your salvation? Are you fearful to share the gospel with others? Ask God to give you the power and the words to tell someone this week about the wonderful Lord who has brought changes to your life. Actively look for opportunities to share your faith in Christ.

DAY 22

Committed to Reaching the Goal

PHILIPPIANS 3:1-14

Key Verses:

Not that I have already obtained all this, or have already been made perfect, but I press on to take hold of that for which Christ Jesus took hold of me. Brothers, I do not consider myself yet to have taken hold of it. But one thing I do: Forgetting what is behind and straining toward what is ahead, I press on toward the goal to win the prize for which God has called me heavenward in Christ Jesus (Philippians 3:12-14).

Today's Focus:

A close relationship with Christ is the greatest goal in life. It is only by committing everything to Him that we realize lasting, genuine fulfillment.

Read: Pray for enlightenment.

    A. Give the reasons for committing everything to Christ.

B. What is the goal for which you should strive?

C. My goal in life is to:

Need: Pray that you may know Christ Jesus more deeply.

My greatest need for today is:

Praise God! He answered my prayer today＿＿＿＿ (date) in this way:

Deed: Pray to encourage others to greater commitment to Christ.

In order to encourage another person to make Christ first in his or her life, I would like to:

*A*pplication

"The more I know Christ, the stronger my commitment to Him will be." With that heartfelt attitude, list the things in your life that you must lay aside in order to gain a greater knowledge of Him. What are some practical steps you can take to press on toward the goal?

DAY 23

My Faith Can Unlock God's Power

DANIEL 6:1-28

Key Verse:

When Daniel was lifted from the den, no wound was found on him, because he had trusted in his God (Daniel 6:23).

Today's Focus:

Every Christian will face times of testing, turmoil, and pain. It's important to remember that when these difficulties come, the Lord is ultimately stronger than anything or anyone. Place your faith in the God of Daniel. He will show His strength.

Read: Praise God He is greater than all.

   A. Describe the attitudes and actions Daniel displayed that revealed inner trust in the Lord.

B. Why did God rescue Daniel?

C. My hope and faith is in God because:

Need: Pray for strength to stand on God's truth.

My greatest need today is:

God's answer to my prayer came on _____ (date) by this means:

Deed: Pray to help others find strength in the Lord.

I will help someone else serve the Lord in the midst of pressure by:

*A*pplication

Are you getting opposition to your faith in God? List the sources of that opposition and how they are affecting you. Pray for courage to continually serve Him regardless of what people say or do to you.

DAY 24

Benefits of Right Actions

GALATIANS 6:1-10

Key Verse:

Let us not become weary in doing good, for at the proper time we will reap a harvest if we do not give up (Galatians 6:9).

Today's Focus:

Every action has consequences. What you sow, you shall reap. As a believer, you are to act in ways that please God so you will reap a harvest of good consequences.

Read: Praise God for He will reward the good things you do.

A. How can Christians help other people?

B. Describe what will happen if you sow to please God.

C. No matter how discouraged or disappointed I may become, I will continue to do good because:

Need: Pray for perseverance to continue to obey the Lord.

My greatest need today is:

It is wonderful to see God answer my prayer today _____ (date). This is what He did:

Deed: Pray for opportunities to do good.

With the guidance of the Holy Spirit, I plan to:

Application

The more you sow, the more you will reap. Ask the Lord to make you sensitive to the needs of others. How will you do good to someone who does not know Christ? Volunteer to get involved in a local church's ministries. Ask God to show you the spiritual gifts He has given you and use them to build others up.

DAY 25

Christ's Resurrection Affects Everything

1 CORINTHIANS 15:1-11, 50-58

Key Verse:

Therefore, my dear brothers, stand firm. Let nothing move you. Always give yourselves fully to the work of the Lord, because you know that your labor in the Lord is not in vain (1 Corinthians 15:58).

Today's Focus:

Real reality is beyond this world. Christ's resurrection proved that. Even though someday you will die, your real life is in Christ. Because He arose, you shall arise. With that hope, you can give yourself totally to the purposes of God for your life.

Read: Thank God that He has defeated death.

A. What are the evidences that Christ arose physically from the grave?

B. How does the message of the risen Christ affect people who believe it?

C. I believe in Christ's resurrection because:

Need: Pray to stand firm for Christ.

My greatest need today is:

On _____ (date) the risen Christ provided the answer to my prayer by:

Deed: Pray for faithfulness to work for the Lord.

Because Christ is alive and lives in me, I desire for Him to guide me to:

*A*pplication

List all the evidence the Bible gives for the Resurrection of Christ. Read Matthew 28, Mark 16, Luke 24, John 20–21, and Acts 1–2. How has the reality of the resurrection affected you?

DAY 26

Overwhelmed by Greatness

ISAIAH 55:1-13

Key Verse:

As the heavens are higher than the earth, so are my ways higher than your ways and my thoughts than your thoughts (Isaiah 55:9).

Today's Focus:

As humans, we are limited in our knowledge and unable to fully understand who God is. He is far beyond our finite minds. Yet the glorious truth is that God, in all His greatness, knows us and rewards those who seek Him!

Read: Pray for insight.

A. Compare the differences between God and you:

What you are like	What God is like

B. What are the results of God's Word going forth from His mouth?

C. Understanding that the Lord is infinitely greater than all humanity makes me feel:

Need: Pray to understand God as much as a human mind can.

My greatest need today is:

God answered my prayer on _____ (date)! Here's how:

Deed: Pray to be led forth by God in joy and peace.

Because God's Word will always accomplish His desires, I am willing to:

*A*pplication

Spend some time in joyful worship today acknowledging God's greatness and majesty. Thank Him for revealing Himself to human beings and for changing your life. Make a list of all the things for which you are thankful. Sing along with the psalmist, "How awesome is the LORD Most High, the great King over all the earth!" (Psalm 47:2).

DAY 27

Humility Now— Glory Later

1 PETER 5:1-11

Key Verses:

Humble yourselves, therefore, under God's mighty hand, that he may lift you up in due time. Cast all your anxiety on him because he cares for you (1 Peter 5:6-7).

Today's Focus:

Humility is not a natural human tendency. Selfishness is the dominant drive in peoples' hearts. But the Chief Shepherd's sheep must be characterized by a humble attitude. He has promised that when you are humble under His mighty hand, He will lift you up—in His way and in His time.

Read: Thank Him that He is the Chief Shepherd.

    A. Describe the people to whom God will give a crown of glory.

B. How can you defeat the Devil?

C. I freely humble myself before God and other people because:

Need: Pray for courage to resist the Devil.

My greatest need today is:

Praise the Chief Shepherd! He answered my prayer today _____ (date) in this way:

Deed: Pray to be an example to God's flock.

I plan to shepherd the flock of God today by:

*A*pplication

List the leadership positions you have at work, in your family, at church, in school, in organizations, and in other situations. How can you lead the people God has entrusted to you in the way God's Word instructs?

DAY 28

Finding Peace Through Prayer

PHILIPPIANS 4:4-13

Key Verses:

Do not be anxious about anything, but in everything, by prayer and petition, with thanksgiving, present your requests to God. And the peace of God, which transcends all understanding, will guard your hearts and minds in Christ Jesus (Philippians 4:6-7).

Today's Focus:

We all desire things. But when we believe the superficial promises of the world, we are rewarded with emptiness and disappointment. On the other hand, God's promises bring genuine fulfillment regardless of our circumstances. Only in Him will we find the satisfying path to personal fulfillment and peace of mind.

Read: Give thanks to the Lord for His peace.

A. Why can you always rejoice?

B. How can you get the peace of God when facing anxiety-producing circumstances?

C. I will rejoice always in the Lord because:

Need: Pray for contentment in all things:

My greatest need today is:

God's answer to my prayer came on _____ (date) by this means:

Deed: Pray that you will be filled with contentment from the Lord.

I will help someone find God's peace by:

*A*pplication

Write down the circumstances and needs that typically make you nervous, anxious, or worried. Next to each entry, write a verse from God's Word that relates to that issue and focuses your mind on God's promises. Pray about these things and leave the results to the Lord. Regardless of the outcome, He will guard your heart with His peace.

DAY
29

New Ways to
Treat People

COLOSSIANS 3:1-17

Key Verse:

*Therefore, as God's chosen people, holy and dearly loved,
clothe yourselves with compassion, kindness, humility,
gentleness and patience* (Colossians 3:12).

Today's Focus:

Every day we come in contact with a variety of people. How
we treat them is strong evidence of the faith that is at work in us.
Whenever you do anything, act in a way that pleases the Lord.
Do it for His glory.

Read: Set your heart on God's ways.

   A. What can you do to show that you are walking in God's
      ways?

B. List the attitudes and actions that you, as a believer in Christ, should avoid.

C. I want to show to the world that Christ is my Lord. So, I will:

Need: Pray to put to death whatever belongs to your earthly nature.

My greatest need today is:

It is thrilling to see God answer my prayer today _____ (date). This is what He did:

Deed: Pray to clothe yourself with compassion, kindness, humility, gentleness, and patience.

With the message of this passage in mind, I will look for an opportunity to:

*A*pplication

Review the list of characteristics of the new life in Christ. In which ones are you succeeding? In which ones are you struggling? Choose one of your weak areas to focus on each day. Ask the Lord to make you stronger in that area and demonstrate your new life in Christ.

DAY 30

Living by the Guidebook

2 TIMOTHY 3:1-17

Key Verses:

All Scripture is God-breathed and is useful for teaching, rebuking, correcting and training in righteousness, so that the man of God may be thoroughly equipped for every good work (2 Timothy 3:16-17).

Today's Focus:

The guidebook for living is the Bible. Understanding and applying God's Word daily is an exciting, lifelong adventure. When you obey what God says, you will never be ashamed or sorry.

Read: Thank God for His Word.

A. Describe people who do not live by God's Word.

B. Why is the Bible the best guidebook for all of life?

C. Even though persecution or suffering may come, I am determined to live by God's Word because:

Need: Pray to live a godly life.

My greatest need today is:

God is good! On _____ (date) He provided the answer to my prayer by:

Deed: Pray to continue in what you have learned from God's Word.

Knowing the value of God's Word, I want to help someone to:

*A*pplication

This 31-Day Experiment is almost over. What will you do to continue your study in God's Word? Look in the back of this book to find practical suggestions for continuing to grow in Christ. Set up a plan for daily meeting with God that will make understanding and applying His Word a lifelong process.

Follow the Leader

MARK 8:27-38

Key Verses:

Then he called the crowd to him along with his disciples and said: "If anyone would come after me, he must deny himself and take up his cross and follow me. For whoever wants to save his life will lose it, but whoever loses his life for me and for the gospel will save it" (Mark 8:34-35).

Today's Focus:

The paradox is that in order to gain your life you have to give it up. God has called us to a life of following Him. Though the process may be painful at times, the benefits outweigh living for self.

Read: Praise the Lord for He is worthy of your total allegiance.

    A. Describe the characteristics and consequences of these two ways of living:

Living for yourself	Living for Christ

B. What does it mean to "lose your life for Christ and for the gospel"?

C. I am a committed follower of Jesus Christ because:

Need: Pray to faithfully follow Him each day.

My greatest need today is:

God answered my prayer on _____ (date). Here's how:

Deed: Pray to be a bold witness and not ashamed of Christ.

Because I love Christ with my whole being, I:

*A*pplication

Draw a scale with numbers 1 to 10. Number 1 represents totally self-centered and 10 represents totally Christ-centered. Put an *X* at the number that represents you in relationship to Jesus right now. Put a *G* next to the number that is your goal for the next month. How are you going to get to that level of commitment to following His leadership? Look at the next sections of this book to get some suggestions.

Faith Goals

Congratulations! You completed this 31-Day Experiment in growing closer to God. For the past month, you have endeavored to develop your personal relationship with the Lord. It has been hard work but well worth the time and effort.

You may have experienced good days as well as bad days, times of growth and times of discouragement. But overall, what type of progress did you make? What lessons did you learn?

It is important to evaluate the results of your studying God's Word and applying it to your life. This will give you a clearer picture of what God has done in your life. It will also help you to continue to grow in your intimacy with Him. Answer the following questions:

1. What five words best describe your relationship with the Lord right now? (Give an explanation for each word.)

(a)

(b)

(c)

(d)

(e)

2. What has changed in your life since you started this experiment?

3. What do you like about your walk with God?

4. What would you like to see change?

5. What specific steps can you take to continue to grow in your faith?

Signed_____ Date_____

Note: Reevaluate your spiritual progress and behavior periodically (such as every six months or each year on your birthday) using a series of questions like those above.

Forging Ahead

꧁

To continue your experiment in developing your walk with the Lord, choose one of these three simple plans. Make it your habit to meet with God each day.

Plan 1: One-a-Day Bible Topics

Go back to the passages you studied each day of this experiment in *Growing Closer to God*. Reread the passage and look for additional interesting and exciting subjects to look into.

You will find suggested ones next to each passage listed below. As you study and pray about these subjects, you will learn much more about God and His perspective on your life. Don't feel limited to these. You may find others as God speaks to you.

Choose one of the words or topics you find in the passage for the day. Get a Bible concordance and dictionary to study the subject. Find out how it is presented throughout the Bible, and determine what its impact should be on your life. Pray for God's guidance and wisdom. Seek to enhance your trust in Him.

Through the inspiration of the Holy Spirit, the Scriptures were written to reveal to you the Lord's character, actions, and commands for you to live according to His eternal principles. Remember, the Bible is God's written revelation of who He is and how He works in this world.

Day and Passage	Words and Topics
1. Matthew 6:25-34	Heavenly Father, Need
2. Psalm 37:1-40	Commit, Delight
3. 1 John 5:1-15	Believe, Eternal
4. Luke 7:36-50	Forgive, Prophet
5. Romans 5:1-11	Hope, Justification
6. Ephesians 3:14-21	Power, Dwell
7. 2 Corinthians 5:11-21	Reconciliation, Ministry
8. Psalm 63:1-11	Soul, Glory
9. Ephesians 5:15-21	Unwise, Wise
10. John 15:1-17	Remain, Fruit
11. Proverbs 3:1-12	Trust, Heart
12. Galatians 5:16-26	Self-control, Spirit
13. 1 John 1:1–2:2	Light, Sin, Atoning Sacrifice
14. Colossians 1:1-14	Inheritance, Knowledge
15. Joshua 1:1-9	Courageous, Successful
16. Romans 8:28-39	Predestine, Conquerors

Day and Passage	Words and Topics
17. James 1:1-18	Mature, Firstfruits
18. 1 Peter 1:3-25	Mercy, Salvation
19. Mark 2:1-12	Faith, Authority
20. Psalm 34:1-10	Extol, Glorify
21. Romans 1:8-25	Preach, God's Wrath
22. Philippians 3:1-14	Righteousness, Goal
23. Daniel 6:1-28	Prayer, Rescue
24. Galatians 6:1-10	Restore, Sowing, and Reaping
25. 1 Corinthians 15:1-11, 50-58	Apostle, Power of Sin
26. Isaiah 55:1-13	Seek, Forsake
27. 1 Peter 5:1-11	Humble, Devil
28. Philippians 4:4-13	Rejoice, Peace
29. Colossians 3:1-17	Compassion, Patience
30. 2 Timothy 3:1-17	Teaching, Persecution
31. Mark 8:27-38	Cross, Ashamed

Here are some guidelines for getting the most out of your study:

(1) Find all the references on the word or topic in a concordance.

(2) From the references listed in the concordance, choose those that seem to apply to your interest and look them up in your Bible. Study the passages that come before and after the verses in order to understand the context.

(3) Follow the cross-references in the verses you are studying if your Bible translation is arranged that way.

(4) List all the biblical references on a sheet of paper. Choose the ones that relate to the subject you are studying. Place a phrase next to each reference that describes the verse. This will help you remember the content of the passage.

(5) Group together the passages that contain similar thoughts and ideas. Notice the emphasis of each group. Outline the material so you can organize all the passages.

(6) What does the Bible say on the topic? Notice the following:

- Commands to obey

- Promises to claim

- Actions to take

- Behavior to avoid

- Principles to believe

(7) Seek to incorporate these biblical truths into your life. Focus on how they will affect your relationship with the Lord, with yourself, and with others. Seek to apply

specifically what you learn each day, and ask God to empower you to live in accordance with that particular part of His Word. For example, if you study the subject of love, have particular people in mind when you ask the Lord to teach you to love, such as: your boss, neighbor, relative, or roommate.

Plan 2: One-a-Day Scripture Meditations

Choose one of these passages to study each day for the next 31 days. Pray for God's guidance. Seek to develop your trust in Him.

1. 2 Chronicles 14:2-15

2. Isaiah 42:1-9

3. Psalm 51:1-9

4. Habakkuk 3:8-19

5. 1 John 4:7-21

6. Luke 15:1-10

7. John 10:22-30

8. Titus 2:11-15

9. Psalm 119:1-16

10. Matthew 13:53-58

11. Jeremiah 17:5-11

12. Mark 9:14-29

13. 2 Corinthians 4:1-18

14. Psalm 139:1-24

15. John 15:16-27

16. James 1:1-18

17. Ephesians 6:10-20

18. Romans 6:1-14

19. Deuteronomy 10:12-22

20. 2 Chronicles 20:1-30

21. 1 Thessalonians 2:1-12

22. 1 Chronicles 29:10-22

23. Lamentations 3:19-33

24. Ephesians 4:7-24

25. Psalm 103:1-18

26. Luke 7:1-10

27. Isaiah 40:27-31

28. Philippians 2:1-11

29. 2 Thessalonians 1:3-12

30. 2 Peter 1:2-11

31. 1 Corinthians 9:19-27

Plan 3: Big Lessons from Little People

1. People are important in God's eyes. There are almost three thousand names of individuals mentioned in the Bible, and God has given us significant information concerning approximately 400 of them. The Lord will teach you many vital lessons when you study their lives. You can be motivated by their strengths and profit from their mistakes.

Below are 15 "little" people mentioned only briefly in the Bible. You can study all that the Bible says about each of them within only 30 to 45 minutes. They will challenge you in a unique way. Choose one a day, and collect all the references to that person from a concordance. Ask God to teach you important lessons He wants you to know as you study them.

    a. Micaiah

    b. Barnabas

    c. Caleb

    d. Stephen

    e. Ruth

    f. Benaiah, the son of Jehoiada

    g. Elizabeth

    h. Hannah

    i. John the Baptist

    j. Titus

    k. Mary of Magdala

    l. Silas

    m. Jonah

    n. Thomas

    o. Philip

2. Reconstruct the person's life. Discover all the information given in the Bible about him or her. Here are some areas

to study about the person (Biblical information may not be available in every area for every person listed).

- Childhood

- Parents and ancestry

- Conversion—if they trusted God

- Traits and qualities—desirable and undesirable

- What they did right or what they did wrong

- Spiritual and social growth

- Relationship with God

- Relationship with others

3. Apply the lessons learned from this study to your own life:

- What can you learn from this person?

- What qualities should you develop?

- What problems should you avoid?

- How does this person help you to know the Lord better?

Continue to seek to know the Lord deeper through expanding your study of His Word each day. Expect Him to open your mind to new understandings of Him and ways to apply His Word. Bible study will become an exciting adventure as you draw closer to His heart. God desires for you to know Him! The more intimate your relationship with Jesus, the deeper the satisfaction He will bring to every area of your life.

Our greatest need, as we have mentioned before, is to know God. When we seek Him above all else, He fulfills our needs in His loving way (Psalm 34:10). Fall in love with Jesus. Feast upon His Word.

> *"I have told you this so that my joy may be in you and that your joy may be complete"* (John 15:11).

My Prayer Journal

(Make additional copies of this page if needed
for more prayer journal space)

Date	Prayer Request	God's Answer

My Prayer Journal

Date	Prayer Request	God's Answer

My Prayer Journal

Date	Prayer Request	God's Answer

How to Lead a Group of People to Grow Closer to God

๘

This 31-Day Experiment (*Growing Closer to God*) has been used by Bible study groups, men's groups, women's groups, families, groups preparing for a missions trip, new-believers groups, Sunday school classes, and entire churches.

Doing this 31-Day Experiment together as a group has lots of benefits:

1. Everyone will be studying the same passages of Scripture during a month.

2. The whole group will be united together in growing closer to God.

3. People will share their prayer requests with others in the group. Everyone will grow in his or her faith as members pray for one another and experience God's answering their prayers.

4. Individuals will see how the Lord is working in one another's lives.

5. Members can encourage one another in their relationships with the Lord and in sharing their faith in God with other people.

Here are some guidelines to start using *Growing Closer to God* with your group:

1. Remind the people of the purpose of your group and the need to deepen their relationships with the Lord.

2. Introduce the 31-Day Experiment goal—to build a habit of spending 20 to 30 minutes each day with the Lord in Bible study, prayer, and application of God's Word to life.

3. Show how the book fits into the purpose for your group. Share ideas and passages of Scripture from the "greatest need" section, and motivate the people to seek to grow closer to God for the next month.

4. There are 31 days of study. Do the first day together as a group, with the leader showing how to do the study. Encourage group members to all start on the same day (preferably the next day) so that each person will always be on the same experiment day. If at all possible, try to meet weekly for an hour to an hour and a half. Therefore, when the next meeting occurs, they will have done six days of the experiment.

5. Plan to do the experiment with your group in five weeks. Each week the group members should start the experiment days on the day after the group meeting. On the day of a group meeting, members should not do the

day's experiment. Rather, they can spend that day reviewing their notes for the previous six days and thanking the Lord for all He has done in their lives.

6. When the group settles on the day they all want to start the experiment, send an e-mail reminder of the date to each person as well as a reminder of the date, time, and place for each weekly meeting. Designate one e-mail address to which people can send e-mails about the things they are learning, prayer requests, and answers to their prayers. Send all the e-mails received to the whole group each day to encourage people to keep doing the experiment. This will help build group unity and spiritual growth.

7. Encourage members to use a Bible dictionary, Bible concordance, or word-study book when they need to understand passages better.

8. Encourage the group to bring their Bibles and their *Growing Closer to God* books to each weekly meeting.

9. When you meet, discuss each day of the previous week's experiment consecutively. Ask people to share with the group what they learned and how it has affected their lives.

10. If your group is large, you may want to divide into smaller subgroups, preferably five to six people in each group. Ask the people in the group or smaller subgroups to call one another during the week to see how each person is doing, answer any questions, and pray together on the phone. In this way, each person will receive several phone calls a week.

11. At the conclusion of each group meeting, pray together, praising the Lord for all He has done and asking Him for consistency to do the experiment faithfully each day. Pray that each person will look forward to meeting with the Lord daily and will experience His presence in their lives during the week.

12. Use the following as a simple format for the weekly meetings.

Weekly Group Participation Outline

Subject: Growing Closer to God

Content: Review the previous six days

Tips for the Leader

1. Prepare your lesson early, asking the Holy Spirit to give you ideas on what to teach and how to draw all the members into the discussion. Be creative. Use a variety of ways to communicate, such as videos, music, drama, and objects—whatever it might take to make the lessons meaningful.

2. Start with an icebreaker as a way of getting to know one another a little better.

3. Begin with the whole group together, interacting on what they learned that week. Or if your group is large, you may want to split up into the subgroups. This will allow a greater number of people to share about their experiences.

4. Find out what hindrances they encountered as they sought to meet with God each day. Discuss how to discipline yourselves to consistently spend time with the Lord in the midst of hectic schedules.

5. Let everyone give input on the first day's topic before going on to the second day's topic.

Questions for Discussion

1. How did your meeting with God each day this past week go?

2. What did you have to do to set aside the 30 minutes each day?

3. What did you learn about walking with God? Loving God? Obeying God?

4. What answers to prayer did you receive? What are you still praying about?

5. What kinds of responses did you receive when you reached out to other people?

Closing

1. Celebrate all that God has done during the past week.

2. Discuss the week ahead and the passages you will be studying. Build interest and excitement for the new things you will encounter and learn.

3. Close in group prayer. Lead in praising the Lord for His working and in asking Him to draw everyone closer to Himself during the week.

4. Motivate the people to pray earnestly for one another during the week. Remind them to phone others and email others about their experiences. Meet with them to discuss how they are doing, and encourage each other to share their faith with people who don't know the Lord personally.

At the end of the five weeks of the experiment:

1. Conclude with a special dinner, or order pizza. Build a fun atmosphere.

2. Make the time a celebration of completing the experiment.

3. Focus attention on the Lord and how wonderful He is.

4. Share testimonies of changed lives and healed relationships.

5. Introduce another 31-Day Experiment. Plan for what you will do next to keep growing in faith and building your group fellowship.

6. Motivate the members to invite their friends to participate in the new experiment. Encourage them to pray for their friends that they might join the group and get involved in growing closer to God.

7. Encourage each person to start their own "Growing Closer to God" group with their friends and neighbors.

Additional Exciting 31-Day Experiments

Now that you have finished a month of studying God's Word and Growing Closer to God, I hope you will want to continue to spend time alone with the risen Lord. He is the Vine from whom you will receive daily life and nourishment. Intimacy with Him continues and increases as you daily remain in Him.

There is a series of 31-Day Experiment books designed to help you develop a consistent devotional time with your heavenly Father. Whether you are a new Christian or have been one for a long time, these 31-Day Experiments will help you strengthen your relationship with Christ. Experience for yourself the joy of discovering God's truth from the Bible.

All the experiment books are designed like the one you have just completed. Each book focuses on a different theme in the Bible and includes relevant passages for you to study.

At the end of each experiment you'll find a number of simple Bible study tools and ideas for further growth. These will help you investigate, on your own, more of the truth that the Holy Spirit wants to teach you.

These books are designed to help you get into God's Word and get God's Word into you.

Knowing God by His Names

When you know God's names, you will never be the same.

Typically, in modern Western culture a name simply identifies one person from another. Beyond perhaps the family-heritage significance of a name, there is little awareness of a name's meaning. However, a person's name in biblical times often referred to a particular trait or characteristic. If you knew the meaning of someone's name, you knew something very important about that person. Individuals usually have one or two given names, but our great Lord has over 200 names! God is the holy Triune God (God the Father, God the Son, and God the Holy Spirit), but He has so many names because each one shines the spotlight on a particular aspect of His infinitely rich character. No one name could tell you everything there is to know about Him.

Each day of this experiment you will study a different name of God. By the end of the book, you will have learned the significance and importance of 31 of His names. Your understanding of God will be enriched and your love for our wonderful Lord will grow deeper. Here are some of the names you will study during the 31 days:

- Father
- Lord Almighty (Jehovah-Sabaoth)
- Prince of Peace
- Lord (Jehovah)
- Most High God
- Living God
- Lord Who Heals (Jehovah-Rophe)
- Son of Man
- Counselor

- King of kings
- LORD Who Provides (Jehovah-Jireh)

As you become on more intimate terms with God by using His names, your prayer life will be transformed. When you have a specific need, you will be able to address God using the name that deals with that situation.

- Anxious? Lean on the Prince of Peace.
- Hurt? Experience comfort from the heavenly Father.
- Guilty? Find forgiveness from the Lamb of God.
- Insecure and fearful? Look to the Rock.
- Looking for direction? Follow the Shepherd.
- Confused? Come to the Light of the World.

In the back of the book, you will find a list of 211 names for God, the characteristics they represent, and a key verse to get you started in learning about each one. In addition, practical instructions will help you unlock the mysteries of God's divine person.

Embrace this exciting approach to developing intimacy with the King of glory. He wants to reveal Himself to you so that you will respond in obedience, faith, love, and worship.

Discovering God's Unique Purpose for You

Do you ever wonder why God made you like you are? What is your purpose for being alive? What do you think about yourself? Regardless of who you are or what you do, this experiment book will help you put your life in a sharper perspective and give you insight into the person God wants you to be.

Are you maximizing your spiritual gifts? Are you using your time wisely? Are you making the most out of your life? Are you pleasing God, the One who made you unique for a unique purpose?

You will study these questions and find biblical answers as you work through the book. You will spend several days studying passages in which God says significant things about how to look at yourself. Your confidence will come from understanding who you are in God's eyes. Then for the rest of the days you will study passages that, if followed, will help you live life to the fullest. You will learn practical things you can do to make your life count for Christ.

This fascinating experiment will give you biblical answers so you can overcome personal doubts and weaknesses. Clearly and powerfully, it will help you see the real truth about yourself from God's point of view. You will receive specific suggestions for living your life to the fullest with significance. Your relationship with the Lord will be enhanced as you spend daily time with Him and discover what the Bible says about how to understand your uniqueness.

Here are some topics you will study to help you develop a biblical self-image:

- What does God say about you?
- Learn to invest your life wisely.
- How to improve yourself.
- Discover and develop your spiritual gifts.
- Getting God's blessings into your daily life.
- Learn to be truly happy.
- What does it mean to "renew your mind"?
- Love like God loves.
- Rejoice in difficulties.
- Maximizing your uniqueness.
- Live with your ultimate future in mind.

These and other important topics will help you develop a positive perspective on yourself and your life.

About the Author
Dick Purnell

Dick Purnell is an internationally known speaker and author. He has spoken in all fifty states in the United States as well as in twelve other countries. He is the Executive Director of Single Life Resources, a division of Campus Crusade for Christ. Dick and his wife, Paula, are on the national speakers' team for FamilyLife Marriage Conferences.

He has authored 13 books, including his latest, *Finding a Lasting Love*. Some of his other books are: *Becoming a Friend and Lover, Free to Love Again, Building a Strong Family, Making a Good Marriage Even Better,* and *Knowing God by His Names.*

A graduate of Wheaton College, Dick holds a master of divinity degree from Trinity International University, as well as a master's in education, specializing in counseling, from Indiana University. He is an adjunct professor at New Life Bible College in Moscow, Russia.

Dick has been featured on many national television shows, including *The Coral Ridge Hour, The 700 Club,* and *The Nashville Hour.* He has been the main guest on many radio programs, such as *FamilyLife Today, Moody Broadcasting, Truths That Transform,* and *America's Family Counselors.*

Bring Dick Purnell to Your Area

Dick Purnell speaks to audiences throughout the United States, Canada, and in many other countries. For information about the wide variety of topics he presents, contact him at:

Dick Purnell
P.O. Box 1166 • Cary, NC 27512 • USA
Phone (919) 363-8000
Web site: www.DickPurnell.com

Other excellent Harvest House Books by Dick Purnell

Finding a Lasting Love

Singles make up 40 percent of the American adult population, and most of them want to find their lifelong mate. Dick Purnell, Executive Director of Single Life Resources, reveals the questions, answers, and insights on dating he shares through conferences, interviews, and articles. Going straight to the heart of the matter, he discusses:

- insights for understanding the opposite sex,
- how to avoid short-circuiting a good relationship,
- suggestions for finding a potential partner, and
- what God's Word says about relationships.

Finding a Lasting Love is beyond a "how to" for the dating reader. It's a biblical exploration of relationships and an invitation to approach dating and life with a healthy, growing faith. Formerly titled *Becoming a Friend & Lover*.

Other 31-Day Experiment Bible Studies

Knowing God by His Names

Singles and Relationships